CRISTIANO RONALDO

This edition published in 2020 by:
The Rosen Publishing Group, Inc.
29 East 21st Street
New York, NY 10010

Additional end matter copyright © 2020 by The Rosen Publishing Group, Inc.

All rights reserved. No part of this book may be reproduced in any form without permission in writing from the publisher, except by a reviewer.

© Carlton Books Ltd, 2020

Cataloging-in-Publication Data

Names: Spragg, Iain.
Title: Cristiano Ronaldo / Iain Spragg.
Description: New York : Rosen YA, 2020. | Series: Soccer superstars
Identifiers: ISBN 9781725340336 (pbk.) | ISBN 9781725340343 (library bound)
Subjects: LCSH: Ronaldo, Cristiano, 1985– —Juvenile literature. | Soccer players—Portugal—Biography—Juvenile literature.
Classification: LCC GV942.7.R626 S67 2019 | DDC 796.334092 B--dc23

Manufactured in the United States of America

SOCCER SUPERSTARS

CRISTIANO RONALDO

Rosen
YA
New York

IAIN SPRAGG

CONTENTS

INTRODUCTION	6
THE EARLY YEARS	8
THE NEXT STEPS	10
HIS BIG BREAKTHROUGH	12
MOVING TO ENGLAND	14
NEW NATIONAL HERO	16
WORLD CUP STAR	18
GREAT MANCHESTER UNITED GOALS	20
MANCHESTER UNITED MILESTONES	22
REAL MADRID MILESTONES	24
AT HOME WITH RONALDO	26
EUROPEAN CHAMPION	28
GREAT REAL MADRID GOALS	30
SUPER SKILLS	32
WINNING LEAGUE CHAMPIONSHIPS	34
PORTUGAL MILESTONES	36
RONALDO IN NUMBERS	38
TRAINING WITH RONALDO	40
RONALDO'S SUPERSTAR TEAMMATES	42
RONALDO AND HIS FANS	44
GREAT PORTUGAL GOALS	46
WORLD TRAVELER	48
EUROPEAN SUPERSTAR	50
RONALDO AND HIS COACHES	52
GLOBAL SUPERSTAR	54
RECORD BREAKER	56
WHAT'S NEXT FOR RONALDO?	58
QUIZ TIME	60
GLOSSARY	62
FOR FURTHER READING	62
INDEX	63

Right: Ronaldo led Portugal to glory in the 2016 UEFA European Championships and his vital contributions included the first penalty in the quarter-final shoot-out victory over Poland.

INTRODUCTION

From his early years on the Portuguese island of Madeira to becoming a superstar in Madrid, the story of Cristiano Ronaldo's career is an incredible soccer blockbuster.

Cristiano Ronaldo is the most famous soccer player on the planet and thanks to his record-breaking performances at top clubs, he is now regarded as the game's greatest player.

The Portuguese magician is soccer's ultimate showman and no one can match the explosive entertainment he provides on the field. Watching Ronaldo is a masterclass in how to destroy the opposition – in style!

Worshipped by his millions of fans and feared by every team he plays against, Ronaldo has come a long way since he joined his first team in his hometown of Funchal as a young boy and began his journey to fame and fortune. It has been a remarkable rise and on the way he has lit up every field he has played on with his incredible skills.

The former Real Madrid star has won every major club trophy in England and Spain, as well as the UEFA Champions League and FIFA Club World Cup – and he added to his incredible collection of winners' medals after leading Portugal to glory at Euro 2016.

He is his country's most capped player and top scorer of all time, a Spanish league record-breaker in front of goal and a five-time winner of the Ballon d'Or, the award given each year to the world's best player.

This book is a celebration of the genius of the Portuguese striker and his amazing achievements. It takes you on a journey that starts in Madeira, passes through Lisbon, Manchester, and Madrid up to his arrival at Juventus in Italy.

The book also looks at Ronaldo's life away from soccer, his family and his fame, as well as how hospital surgery helped him overcome a heart problem as a teenager.

You don't have to be a Real Madrid or Juventus supporter to love Ronaldo's unique talents and this book is the ultimate guide to the ultimate player.

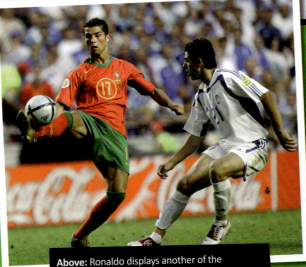

Above: Ronaldo displays another of the trademark tricks that have made him a global superstar.

Below: No one has scored more international goals for Portugal than Ronaldo.

Above: Ronaldo won his third UEFA Champions League final in 2016, his second for Real Madrid—which had 11—and scored with the final attempt in the penalty shoot-out against Atlético Madrid.

THE EARLY YEARS

The star was an unruly student at school! But away from the classroom it was obvious he had a very special talent.

Ronaldo was born on February 5, 1985, on the Portuguese island of Madeira. He was christened Cristiano Ronaldo dos Santos Aveiro by his parents because his father, José, was a big fan of an old Hollywood actor named Ronald Reagan. When Ronaldo was born, Reagan had become president of the USA.

The family lived in the city of Funchal on the south coast of the island. José worked as a gardener for the local council while his mother, Maria, was a cook. They were not rich, but the lack of money only helped to bring Ronaldo and his two older sisters, Elma and Liliana Cátia, and his big brother, Hugo, closer together.

Above: Nine-year-old Ronaldo's identity card for the 1994–95 season, when he played for Clube de Futebol Andorinha in Funchal, Madeira.

"I was brought up with nothing," Ronaldo said. "We were very poor. I had no toys and no Christmas presents. I shared a room with my brother and two sisters and my parents slept in the other. It was a small space but I didn't mind. I'm incredibly close to my brother and two sisters and we loved being together. For us it was normal, it was all we knew. Everybody around us lived the same way and we were happy."

When he was eight years old, Ronaldo joined the junior team at his local club, Andorinha. But while his first soccer coaches were amazed by his skills, his school teachers were not as impressed. "I was not thick but I was not interested in school," he said. "I was expelled after I threw a chair at the teacher. He disrespected me. When I got to 14 … I thought I was maybe good enough at that time to play semi-professionally."

His family agreed with him and decided that he should concentrate on his soccer rather than his studies. Ronaldo was now on his way to becoming the world's greatest soccer player.

Above: Ronaldo grew up in a poor family but enjoyed a happy childhood on the Portuguese island of Madeira.

Below: Ronaldo has become the game's greatest player.

THE NEXT STEPS

The superstar began to make a big impression in his home country of Portugal, despite a frightening problem with his health.

Ronaldo spent two seasons with Andorinha, but it was already obvious that the boy was a special talent. So in 1995 he switched clubs, joining Nacional, in his hometown of Funchal. He was still only 10 years old, but this move had a big effect on his career.

In his first season at Nacional, Ronaldo's Under-11 team won their league title and word was beginning to spread about the team's skinny midfielder with the outrageous skills. "People knew I was a talented kid," Ronaldo said.

The talent spotters at big club Sporting Lisbon, based in Portugal's capital city, had heard of him and he was invited to the club for a three-day trial. It meant leaving the island of Madeira and heading to the Portuguese mainland, but Ronaldo was determined to take his big chance. After the trial, Sporting Lisbon decided to offer him an apprenticeship.

Ronaldo continued to impress the coaching staff at Sporting, but at the age of 15 he was suddenly diagnosed with a serious heart problem and the club decided he needed an operation to cure it.

The problem was that his heart was beating too fast, even when he wasn't running. His mother Maria said, "The people in charge at Sporting called me and I went to Portugal where I had to sign some papers so he could be treated in hospital. I was worried because he might have to give up playing football. But the treatment went well and after a few days he was back training again."

Luckily, Ronaldo made a complete recovery and starred for Portugal at the European Under-17 Championship held in Denmark in 2002, starting in the group games against France and Ukraine. When he got back to his club, he was promoted to the reserves. So the teenager had almost made it to the first team and a few months later took the final step to become a full senior player.

Above: From his first days at Sporting Clube de Portugal (aka Sporting Lisbon), Ronaldo took his pre-training stretching exercises very seriously.

Below: Sporting's fans, especially at their Estádio José Alvalade home, are among Portugal's most passionate.

10

Above: Even in training, Ronaldo was all business because he knew that perfecting his technique would take him a long way.

HIS BIG BREAKTHROUGH

Just a few months after his 17th birthday, Ronaldo made the headlines with a sensational league debut for Sporting Lisbon.

Although everyone in Lisbon knew just how talented Ronaldo was, he was not yet well known outside the city. But all that changed in October 2002 when the teenager was given his senior debut for the club.

The Sporting manager, Laszlo Boloni, decided Ronaldo was ready to perform with all the top professionals and put him in the team to play against Moreirense in a Portuguese Primeira Liga game at the club's home ground, the Estádio José Alvalade.

The time had come for Ronaldo to show the world his magic and the 17-year-old did not disappoint. Sporting won the match – and Ronaldo scored twice!

His first goal came in the first half after he picked up the ball inside the Moreirense half and set off on an amazing run. His speed took him past one sliding tackle and when a second player closed in on him, he produced an outrageous stepover, which left the embarrassed defender behind him. The Moreirense goalkeeper rushed out, but Ronaldo did not panic and unleashed a deadly low shot that hit the back of the net.

His second goal came in second-half injury time. Sporting were awarded a free-kick near the corner flag and as the ball came sailing into the area, it was Ronaldo who jumped above the Moreirense defense to head home and seal the team's 3–0 victory.

Above: Five months after his 17th birthday, Ronaldo saw first-team action for Sporting Lisbon in preseason friendlies.

A star had been born. Every soccer fan in Portugal had now heard of the youngster from Madeira and his life would never be the same again.

Ronaldo made 24 more Primeira Liga appearances for his club during the 2002–03 season as Sporting finished third in the table. He also scored twice in three Portuguese Cup games. He was suddenly the hottest property in Portuguese soccer and although he didn't yet realize it, it would not be long before one of the most biggest and famous clubs in the world was knocking on Sporting's door trying to sign the teenager.

Above: A month after his first-team debut for Sporting, Ronaldo was showing off his ball skills to Marítimo defenders Albertino (*left*) and Joel.

MOVING TO ENGLAND

After just one full season with Sporting, Ronaldo was on his way to Old Trafford to play for the mighty Manchester United.

It was not long after Ronaldo's amazing debut for Sporting that some of Europe's top clubs began to take notice of the teenager. Both Liverpool and Barcelona were interested and Ronaldo even met Arsenal manager Arsene Wenger at the club's training ground to discuss joining the Gunners.

The race for his signature was heating up, but there could only be one winner – Manchester United.

What really sealed the deal was a match between Sporting and United in the summer of 2003 in Lisbon. The game was staged to celebrate the opening of Sporting's new stadium and Ronaldo was the man of the match as his Portuguese team beat the Premier League champions 3–1.

Six days later United signed him, handing the 18-year-old the number seven shirt worn by David Beckham the previous season. Manager Sir Alex Ferguson admitted it was Ronaldo's dazzling display in the match in Portugal that convinced him he was going to become a star.

"He is an extremely talented footballer, a two-footed attacker who can play anywhere up front," Ferguson said after the deal was done. "After we played Sporting last week the lads in the dressing room talked about him constantly and on the plane back from the game they urged me to sign him. That's how highly they rated him. He is one of the most exciting young players I've ever seen."

It was the start of a brilliant six seasons for Ronaldo in England in which he won eight major trophies, was voted the best player in Europe in 2008, and scored more than 100 goals for the Red Devils. Old Trafford worshipped their Portuguese playmaker and Ronaldo repeatedly repaid the fans with some of the most magical soccer they had ever seen.

Above: Ronaldo takes the ball away from Nicky Butt in summer 2003; within a week they were Manchester United teammates.

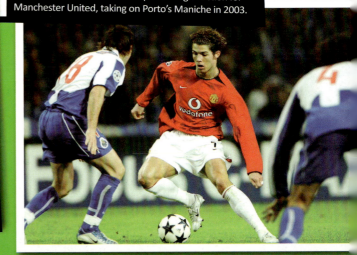

Below: Ronaldo in UEFA Champions League action for Manchester United, taking on Porto's Maniche in 2003.

"He surpassed all the other great ones I coached at Manchester United. And I had many."
Sir Alex Ferguson

Above: Ronaldo celebrates another goal for United, helping them to knock out FC Porto in the 2008–09 UEFA Champions League quarter-final.

NEW NATIONAL HERO

Football is Portugal's number one sport and in Ronaldo the country has a special player to make the nation proud.

Before Ronaldo burst onto the scene more than 10 years ago, the two most famous names in the history of Portuguese football were two players called Eusébio and Luís Figo. Both were amazing flair players who won all the big trophies at club level and gave some incredible performances for the national team.

Ronaldo, however, has eclipsed them both and is now recognized as the greatest player Portugal has ever produced.

It all began when the then Sporting Lisbon star was given his international debut as a teenager in a match against Kazakhstan in 2003. He played for just 45 minutes, but he was in the starting line-up for his second cap two months later when Portugal smashed Albania 5–3. It was already obvious Portugal had unearthed a new hero.

Above: Cristiano Ronaldo was just 18 when he won his first cap for Portugal against Kazakhstan in 2003.

His first full 90 minutes of action came during Euro 2004 and the dramatic penalty shootout win over England in Lisbon in the quarter-finals. Although Portugal were ambushed in the final by Greece, Ronaldo was now a firm fixture in the team.

Left: Ronaldo was on target during the 2004 Olympic Games against Morocco.

16

Since then the striker has surpassed both Eusébio and Figo and rewritten the Portuguese record books.

By the end of the 2015–16 season, and Portugal's amazing victory in Euro 2016, Ronaldo had won 133 caps for his country. Figo had held the record with 127 appearances, but Ronaldo passed that milestone when Portugal faced Austria in the second game of European Championship finals.

He also had netted a staggering 61 international goals by then, easily beating the previous Portuguese record of 47 set by former teammate Pauleta.

The international records set by the remarkable Ronaldo do not stop there. No one has played in more European Championship finals games (21) than Ronaldo or scored more goals in the finals (9). He is also the only player to score in four Euro finals tournaments (2004, 2008, 2012, and 2016).

It's an awesome list of achievements from Portugal's greatest ever soccer player and with time still on his side, he has the chance to smash even more records.

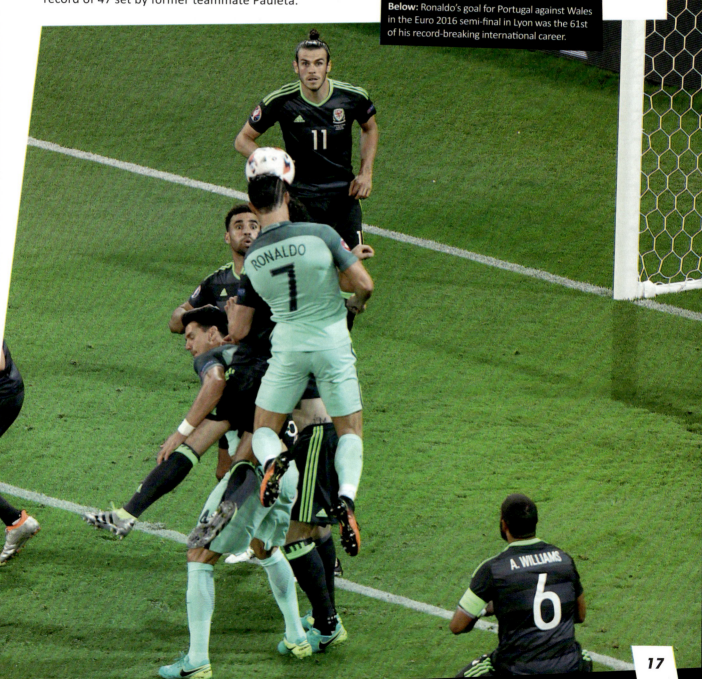

Below: Ronaldo's goal for Portugal against Wales in the Euro 2016 semi-final in Lyon was the 61st of his record-breaking international career.

WORLD CUP STAR

Having played in four World Cups, Ronaldo is one of international soccer's biggest stars.

It is every player's dream to play in the World Cup and Ronaldo has already done it four times with Portugal, displaying his dazzling skills to TV audiences all around the world. The soccer magician was born to play in the sport's most famous event.

It was Ronaldo's seven goals in qualifying that booked Portugal's place in the 2006 World Cup. They were unbeaten on their way to the Finals and went on to win Group D.

Inspired by Ronaldo's attacking play, everyone was talking about Portugal as potential World Cup winners, and when they beat Holland 1–0 in the Last 16, there was real hope that the team could go all the way.

England stood in their way in the quarter-finals, but the match was scoreless so a penalty shootout beckoned. Ronaldo took the all-important final kick and won the match.

Although the semi-final against France brought heartbreak, as Zinedine Zidane scored the only goal of the game to knock Portugal out, Ronaldo and his nation's performances were recognized when they were given the FIFA award for the Most Entertaining Team.

In 2008, Ronaldo was made Portugal captain at the age of just 23, only two months before the start of qualifying for the 2010 World Cup in South Africa. He rose to the challenge brilliantly.

Portugal were drawn in a tough group that had both Brazil and the Ivory Coast in it, but Ronaldo made sure they reached the knockout stages, scoring Portugal's seventh and final goal in their 7–0 demolition of North Korea in Cape Town. Portugal then lost to European champions Spain, 1–0, in the last 16.

Portugal were back in World Cup action in 2014 thanks to four Ronaldo goals in qualifying and four more that destroyed Sweden in the playoffs, but despite his 50th international goal in the group game against Ghana, the Portuguese narrowly missed out on qualification for the knockout phase on goal difference.

In the 2018 World Cup in Russia, Portugal finished second in their group to Spain. They were eliminated in the last 16 after falling to Uruguay, 2–1. During the tournament, Ronaldo broke Ferenc Puskás's record for most international goals scored by a European player.

Above: Ronaldo scored the winner for Portugal against Ghana at the 2014 World Cup.

Left: Ronaldo celebrates after helping Portugal to knock out England in the 2006 FIFA World Cup quarter-final.

Below: Ronaldo dances past Brazilian defender Juan during the goalless draw in the group stage of the 2010 FIFA World Cup in South Africa.

GREAT MANCHESTER UNITED GOALS

Ronaldo hit an incredible 118 goals in England in just 292 appearances for the mighty Manchester United. These are five of his very best.

Above: Ronaldo blasts the ball toward goal to give Manchester United a 1–0 win over FC Porto in the UEFA Champions League quarter-final.

MANCHESTER UNITED 2 PORTSMOUTH 0
PREMIER LEAGUE, JANUARY 30, 2008

Ronaldo is the most deadly player in the world with a long-range free-kick and this sensational 30-yard effort at Old Trafford was one of his very best. It flew like a laser-guided missile past Portsmouth keeper David James and into the top right corner of the net.

MANCHESTER UNITED 4 ASTON VILLA 0
PREMIER LEAGUE, MARCH 29, 2008

A beautiful goal that few other players could have dreamed of scoring, Ronaldo pounced on a loose ball in the penalty area and then cheekily back-heeled the ball behind his left leg, through a crowd of confused defenders and into the back of the net.

CHELSEA 1 MANCHESTER UNITED 1
CHAMPIONS LEAGUE, MAY 21, 2008

The best players always save their best for the very biggest matches and Ronaldo did the business in the UEFA Champions League Final in Moscow when he rose above the Chelsea defense to punch home Wes Brown's cross with a thumping header. United went on to win the trophy after a penalty shootout.

Above: Rising high above the watching Chelsea defense, Ronaldo heads Manchester United's goal in the 2008 UEFA Champions League Final.

PORTO 0 **MANCHESTER UNITED 1**
CHAMPIONS LEAGUE, APRIL 15, 2009

United needed to win to reach the semi-finals of the Champions League and Ronaldo delivered when it mattered most with a truly spectacular winner, a thunderbolt from 40 yards out that almost burst the net as it screamed past the stunned Porto keeper. Even Ronaldo's teammates could not believe what they had just seen.

ARSENAL 1 **MANCHESTER UNITED 3**
CHAMPIONS LEAGUE, MAY 5, 2009

Another utterly unstoppable free-kick, Ronaldo unleashed this magnificent effort against Arsenal in the Champions League semi-final, blasting home from a wide angle past the wall and beating Gunners' keeper Manuel Almunia for pace and power at his near post.

MANCHESTER UNITED MILESTONES

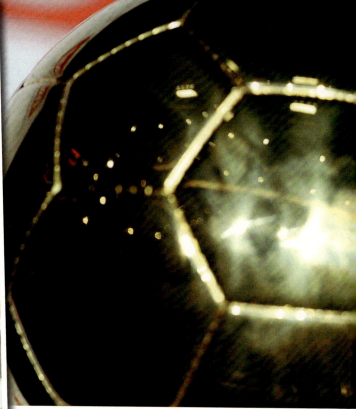

Above: Ronaldo shows off the FA Cup after he had scored the opening goal of the 2004 final against Millwall, a match United won 3–0.

AUGUST 16, 2003
Ronaldo makes his debut for Manchester United, coming off the bench to replace Nicky Butt after 61 minutes in a 4–0 demolition of Bolton Wanderers at Old Trafford.

MAY 22, 2004
Scores the opening goal in a 3–0 win over Millwall in the FA Cup Final to lift his first trophy with the Red Devils. He went on to win three Premier League titles (2006–07, 2007–08, 2008–09), two League Cups (2006 and 2009), the Champions League (2008) and the FIFA Club World Cup (2008) with United.

AUGUST 9, 2005
Scores the third goal in a 3–0 victory for United in their UEFA Champions League qualifier against Hungarian side Debrecen, his first-ever goal in Europe.

APRIL 1, 2007
Ronaldo is named the Football Writers' Association Footballer of the Year. He had already been voted the PFA Young Player, Players' Player and Fans' Player of the Year and became the first soccer player ever to hold all four awards at the same time.

MARCH 19, 2008
Captains Manchester United for the first time in his career at the age of 23, scoring both of the goals in the Red Devils' comfortable 2-0 victory against Bolton Wanderers at Old Trafford.

Above: The Portuguese star was just 23 years old when he was voted European Footballer of the Year and received the UEFA Ballon d'Or.

NOVEMBER 15, 2008
Scores his 100th United goal in a 5–0 thrashing of Stoke City.

MAY 11, 2008
Scores in a 2–0 victory away at Wigan. It's his 31st Premier League goal of the season, a feat which earned him the European Golden Shoe award.

DECEMBER 2, 2008
Ronaldo collects the Ballon d'Or for the first time, the award given to the best soccer player in Europe, beating Lionel Messi into second place in the vote.

JANUARY 12, 2009
Ronaldo becomes the first Premier League player ever to be voted FIFA World Player of the Year.

MAY 10, 2009
Scores in a 2–0 defeat of Manchester City at Old Trafford, his 118th and final goal for United in 292 appearances for the club.

DECEMBER 22, 2009
Collects the first-ever FIFA Puskas Award for the best goal of the year, his 40-yard thunderbolt against FC Porto in the UEFA Champions League.

REAL MADRID MILESTONES

Above: Ronaldo celebrates after scoring one of his five goals in the 9–1 victory over Grenada in La Liga on April 5, 2015.

JULY 1, 2009
Joins Real Madrid from Manchester United for world-record fee of $131.5 million (£80 million).

APRIL 20, 2011
Scores the winner in extra-time of the Copa del Rey Final against Barcelona to lift his first trophy as a Madrid player.

MAY 21, 2011
Scores twice in an 8–1 demolition of Almeira in the final league game of the season. His double strike takes his tally for the season to 40, the first player in La Liga history to reach this number.

MAY 2, 2012
The striker finds the back of the net in a 3–0 away win against Athletic Bilbao, a result that gives Real Madrid the Spanish league title for a record-breaking 32nd time. He wins the La Liga player of the season.

MAY 13, 2012
Scores in a 4–1 league victory against Real Mallorca, a goal that makes Ronaldo the first player in the history of La Liga to score against every other team in the division in a single season.

MAY 8, 2013
Scores 200th goal for the club, against Malaga, to reach a double-century of strikes quicker than any of the other great players in the history of the club.

MAY 24, 2014
Ronaldo scores in the 4–1 win over Atlético Madrid in the UFEA Champions League final. His 17th goal in 11 appearances breaks the previous Champions League/European Cup single-season record of 14.

AUGUST 12, 2014
Scores twice in Real Madrid's 2–0 victory over Sevilla in the UEFA Super Cup.

Above: Ronaldo became Real's record goal scorer in October 2015 to cement his status as a Bernabéu legend.

AUGUST 28, 2014
Wins UEFA Best Player in Europe award.

MARCH 10, 2015
Scores two goals in Real's 3–4 home defeat to Schalke in the Champions League to become the outright top scorer in all UEFA competitions (with 78 goals) and joins Lionel Messi as the Champions League's all-time top scorer.

MAY 2, 2015
Scores 29th hat-trick of Real Madrid – against Sevilla – to break Alberto di Stefano's club record.

SEPTEMBER 12, 2015
Scores five goals in a game for the second time, in a 6–0 demolition of Espanyol, taking him to 230 league goals in 203 games and past Raúl's previous club record of 228.

OCTOBER 17, 2015
Becomes Madrid's all-time leading scorer in all competitions, with 324 goals, when he nets against Levante at the Bernabéu.

APRIL 2, 2016
Nets a hat-trick in the Champions League semi-final second leg against Wolfsburg. His treble makes him the tournament's top scorer for the fourth consecutive season.

MAY 28, 2016
Converts the decisive penalty in the Champions League final shoot-out against Atlético Madrid as Real Madrid win the Cup for the 11th time.

MAY 17, 2017
Passes Jimmy Greaves as the top all-time goal scorer in Europe's top five leagues with his 367th and 368th goals.

DECEMBER 7, 2017
Wins the Ballon d'Or for the fifth time and second straight year.

MAY 26, 2018
Real Madrid wins the Champions League for the third straight year, becoming the first team to do so. Ronaldo scores the most goals of any player during the tournament for the sixth straight year.

AT HOME WITH RONALDO

When he's not showing off his unbelievable skills on the field, Ronaldo enjoys a quiet life away from the spotlight.

It's not easy being one of the most famous people on the planet and Ronaldo gets away from the pressures of soccer by spending his free time with family and friends. He became a father in July 2010 when Cristiano Ronaldo Junior was born and the star insists there is nowhere he would rather be than at home with his son.

"I am a very private person and I am down-to-earth," he said in 2011. "My family comes first – my son is the most important thing in my life. I salute him in the crowd every time I score a goal. After that it's the football that matters most to me. Money comes after that."

Ronaldo now has three younger children as well: twins Eva and Mateo, born in June 2017, and Alana, born in November 2017.

One thing that has always marked out Cristiano as a special player is his absolute dedication to soccer. He would much rather stay at home, looking after himself, than go out with his Bernabéu teammates.

"Half the boys like to go to the disco. They like to party hard, they like to try to impress girls with champagne. But it's better to train hard and do well."

Ronaldo's father sadly died in 2005, but he remains very close to his mother, his sisters, and his brother. Despite all the money he earns, he is not that interested in cash. He has said he bought his mother and sisters houses.

"My brother runs my nightclubs and various bars," he said. "I also own a hotel. But money hasn't changed me – I'm still the same person. I have my circle of friends, my club. People who've been with me a long time. I look after these people."

Ronaldo's fans got a rare glimpse inside his home, just outside Madrid, in 2016 when he let in a camera crew and it made for fascinating viewing as we got to see how the star lives away from the spotlight.

There was of course a soccer field in his backyard but more surprising were a leopard skin duvet cover, statue of Buddha, and, because it was December, Nativity scene set up by his private swimming pool.

One room is for all his trophies and winners' medals, but Ronaldo revealed the most important room in the house was his bedroom, "because to perform good and be at a good level you have to rest good."

Below: Despite his massive fame and fortune, Ronaldo has always remained incredibly close to his mother Maria.

26

> "I always had a gift. I was shown the skills and I am a fantastic footballer but I do believe God gave me the gift."

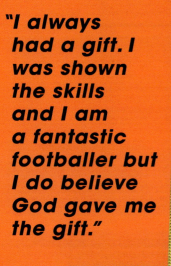

Below: Ronaldo poses with his son beneath a statue of himself during the unveiling ceremony in his hometown in Funchal in December 2014.

Above: The Portuguese legend shows off the 2014 FIFA Ballon d'Or trophy he has just received. He is accompanied by his young son Cristiano, with whom he spends as much time as possible.

EUROPEAN CHAMPION

Ronaldo made his European Championship finals debut in 2004 and, 12 years later, he captained Portugal to glory in Euro 2016 in France.

Ronaldo first played for his country in August 2003, when he came off the bench against Kazakhstan. His Manchester United debut had come only four days before, against Bolton Wanderers, and was the start of an exciting new phase of his incredible career.

Less than a year later he was playing in Euro 2004, which was held in Portugal, and, although he was still only a teenager, Ronaldo was in amazing form as the hosts went all the way to the final.

His goal in the semi-final win over Holland was crucial and despite Portugal losing in the final to Greece, Ronaldo was named in the UEFA All-Star Team of the competition alongside star names like Zinedine Zidane, Frank Lampard, Michael Ballack, and fellow Portuguese Luís Figo.

Above: Ronaldo celebrates after scoring against the Czech Republic in the 2008 European Championship finals.

Ronaldo scored an incredible seven goals in the qualifying matches as Portugal reached Euro 2008 in Switzerland and Austria. For the first time, he was handed the number seven shirt for a big tournament by manager Luiz Felipe Scolari.

A goal and a man-of-the-match performance in a 3–1 group stage win over the Czech Republic sent Portugal into the knockout phase, but Ronaldo could not stop Germany winning the quarter-final tie.

Ronaldo's third appearance in the European Championships came in 2012 in Poland and Ukraine and Portugal went into their final group game against Holland needing a win to stay in the tournament. Step forward Ronaldo with two goals to save the day.

Left: Ronaldo's first major tournament for Portugal was Euro 2004.

He was on target again with the only goal of the game against the Czech Republic in the quarter-finals. But there was heartbreak in the semi-final against Spain as Portugal lost on penalties. However, Ronaldo had shown his superstar status and was again named in the UEFA Team of the Tournament.

Ronaldo's greatest moment, however, came in 2016 as Portugal won their first major trophy after beating hosts France in the final in Paris in extra time. Although he played in all seven games at Euro 2016, a bad knee injury sadly forced him off early in the final. An extra-time goal from Éder meant Ronaldo had finally won the trophy he'd always dreamed of.

"I'm so happy," he said. "This is something I have wanted for a long time now, ever since 2004. The Portuguese people deserve this; our players deserve this. This is one of the happiest moments of my career. I've always said I wanted to win a trophy with the national team and make history."

Below: Ronaldo scored three goals to help Portugal become European champions for the first time.

GREAT REAL MADRID GOALS

The Portuguese player has been deadly in front of goal since he signed for Real Madrid in 2009 and here are five of his most spectacular efforts.

VILLAREAL 0 **REAL MADRID 2**
LA LIGA, SEPTEMBER 23, 2009

Ronaldo's blistering pace was incredible as he spun away from a desperate Villareal tackle on the halfway line and raced towards goal. His speed took him past another attempted tackle before he fired home into the bottom right corner.

REAL MADRID 6 VILLAREAL 2
LA LIGA, FEBRUARY 21, 2010

Even with his reputation for amazing free-kicks, few expected the Portuguese star to score against Villareal as he carefully placed the ball 35 yards (32 m) out from goal. But he, of course had other ideas, launching a dazzling drive from the left that sailed beautifully into the top right corner.

RAYO VALLECANO 0 **REAL MADRID 1**
LA LIGA, FEBRUARY 26, 2012

A wonder goal worthy of winning any game, there seemed no danger when Rayo cleared a Real corner and Ronaldo was forced to retreat away from goal with the ball. Cue an outrageous, deadly back-heel that completely surprised the Vallecano defenders and keeper.

Above: Ronaldo is congratulated by Marcelo after his brilliant goal at Villareal's Madrigal in September 2009.

Right: Ronaldo's amazing back-heel against Rayo Vallecano in 2012 was simply world class.

REAL MADRID 2 BARCELONA 1
SPANISH SUPER CUP, AUGUST 29, 2012

The highlight of this remarkable goal was the amazing back-heel flick in the middle of the field over Gerard Piqué that left the Barcelona defender stranded before Ronaldo smashed an unstoppable drive past Víctor Valdés to win the Spanish Super Cup.

BORUSSIA DORTMUND 2 REAL MADRID 2
CHAMPIONS LEAGUE, SEPTEMBER 27, 2016

This stunning team goal featured all of Madrid's attacking stars and was finished off in style by Ronaldo. Gareth Bale's trademark burst from into the box was followed by a back-heel to slice open the Dortmund defense and there was Ronaldo, in the right place at the right time, to smash the ball into the bottom corner.

Below: Ronaldo finishes off a fantastic move against Barcelona with the winning kick in 2012 Spanish Super Cup.

Above: Ronaldo's strike against Dortmund in Germany was the 93rd goal of his Champions League career.

31

SUPER SKILLS

Ronaldo's amazing array of tricks and awesome talents are what makes him the world's greatest player.

IN THE AIR
Loads of Ronaldo's goals come from headers and there are few players who can jump as high or hang in the air as long before he thumps home another headed effort. The power he is able to generate with his snap headers is awesome.

FABULOUS FLIP FLAP
One of the most outrageous tricks in his box, Ronaldo's "Flip Flap" gives defenders sleepless nights. First he moves the ball away with the outside of his shoe and when the defender makes his move, he rolls his studs over the ball and in the blink of an eye shifts it back with his instep and away from the tackle.

NEED FOR SPEED
Ronaldo is blessed with incredible speed and his ability to race past players anywhere on the field is one of the big reasons he is such a handful. Only the very quickest defenders can live with him.

SUPERB SHOOTING

His long-range shooting is so good that every time he gets past the halfway line, the alarm bells start ringing for defenders. Ronaldo can hit a devastating range of shots, from the inswinger and the flat drive to the outswinger and the dipper.

FANTASTIC FREE-KICKS

Ronaldo has rewritten the rule book when it comes to free-kicks and there's almost no distance from which he can't go for goal. No one can get as much dip and swerve on the ball as the Portuguese athlete, but he also has the raw power needed to blast it past the keeper.

DAZZLING DRIBBLING

Speed alone is not enough to make a world-class player and it is Ronaldo's incredible dribbling at full speed that sets him apart. He bamboozles defenders with his unbelievable balance and ability to keep the ball just inches away from his feet.

THE STEP-OVER

Fans have lost count of the number of confused defenders Ronaldo has beaten with his devastating step-over, sending defenders first one way and then the other before racing past them as they desperately try not to fall over.

33

WINNING LEAGUE CHAMPIONSHIPS

Ronaldo has been a key part of every team he has played in both in England and Spain. So he knows all about getting his hands on the most important trophies.

Only the most talented teams get to become league champions and Ronaldo has been the star in four of these sides, winning the Premier League three times in a row with Manchester United and winning La Liga twice with Real Madrid.

His first Premier League triumph came in the 2006–07 season. After scoring on the opening day in a 5–1 demolition of Fulham at Old Trafford, there was no stopping him. He finished the campaign as the Red Devils' top scorer with 17 league goals and Sir Alex Ferguson's side were champions again.

Ronaldo was even more deadly in 2007–08 as United defended their title. It was a close race with Chelsea all the way through the season, but his two priceless goals in a 4–1 defeat of West Ham United and another in a 2–0 victory away against Wigan Athletic in the last two games were enough to see off the Londoners' challenge.

United made it a magnificent hat-trick of titles in 2008–09 and once again Ronaldo was the difference as he again finished top scorer for the club with 18 great goals, more than a quarter of the team's Premier League total. He was definitely now an Old Trafford legend.

Real Madrid were desperate for Ronaldo to bring some of that magic to the Bernabéu after his record transfer in the summer of 2009 and he delivered just that in the 2011–12 season.

Barcelona had won three La Liga titles in a row but Ronaldo almost single-handedly brought that run to an end with a record-breaking season that saw Real Madrid crowned champions, nine points ahead of their big rivals.

The striker scored an unbelievable 46 times in 38 games – more than a third of Real Madrid's total of 121 La Liga goals.

In the 2016–17 season, Ronaldo won his second La Liga championship with Real Madrid. He was the team's top scorer with 25 goals during the season, good enough for third in the league.

On July 10, 2018, Ronaldo signed with Juventus, historically the most successful team in Italy's Serie A.

Right: Ronaldo's 46 goals in 38 La Liga games in 2011–12 saw Real Madrid crowned champions of Spain.

PORTUGAL MILESTONES

AUGUST 20, 2003
Makes debut for Portugal, aged just 18 years and 7 months, against Kazakhstan.

JUNE 12, 2004
Scores in Portugal's 2–1 group stage defeat against Greece in Porto, his first international goal.

AUGUST 15, 2004
Scores for Portugal in a 2–1 group stage win over Morocco at the Athens Olympic Games.

JUNE 17, 2006
Ronaldo is on target from the penalty spot in a 2–0 victory over Iran in Frankfurt, his first World Cup Finals goal.

FEBRUARY 6, 2007
Captains Portugal for the first time as the team beat Brazil 2–0 in a friendly at the Emirates Stadium. When Carlos Queiroz is appointed coach in July 2008 Ronaldo becomes the permanent captain.

OCTOBER 16, 2012
By playing against Northern Ireland in a World Cup qualifier in Porto, Ronaldo joins Luís Figo and Fernando Couto as the only Portuguese players to win 100 caps.

NOVEMBER 19, 2013
A hat-trick from the Real Madrid star in the second leg of their playoff against Sweden sends Portugal to the 2014 World Cup. The goals take Ronaldo's total for Portugal in 2013 to 10, the best international haul of his career so far.

MARCH 5, 2014
The striker scores twice in a 5–1 friendly victory against Cameroon. It takes him to a total of 49 international goals and makes him Portugal's all-time leading scorer, breaking Pauleta's previous record of 47.

JUNE 26, 2014
The striker scores the winner in the group stage match against Ghana in the 2014 FIFA World Cup in Brazil, the 50th goal of his remarkable international career.

JUNE 18, 2016
Makes his 128th international appearance against Austria in Paris to become Portugal's most-capped player.

JULY 6, 2016
His goal against Wales in the Euro 2016 semi-final, sees Ronaldo match Michel Platini's record of nine in the European Championship finals.

OCTOBER 7, 2016
Ronaldo scores four goals in one international game for the first time as Portugal hammer Andorra 6–0 in a World Cup qualifier.

Below: Ronaldo beats the lunging Mikael Antonsson of Sweden in Portugal's 3–2 2014 World Cup qualifying playoff win.

Above: Ronaldo overtook Luís Figo's record of 127 Portugal caps against Austria at Euro 2016.

RONALDO IN NUMBERS

Cristiano Ronaldo breaks soccer records with a regularity that would impress a Swiss clockmaker. Here are some key numbers in the career of the man known as CR7.

Below: Ronaldo has been deadly in front of goal ever since he signed for Madrid.

9
The number of minutes it took the striker to smash three goals past Granada in April 2015, the fastest hat-trick in Real Madrid history.

158
The incredible number of fans, in millions, who were following Ronaldo on Instagram by 2019.

154
Ronaldo's total number of caps for Portugal through 2018.

450
The total number of La Liga goals he had scored for Real Madrid in his nine seasons there, 2009–18.

658
His amazing tally of goals for club and country by the end of the 2017–18 season.

12
The number of times of Ronaldo has been named in the prestigious FIFA FIFPro World XI

2019
The year in which Ronaldo signed for his third major European club, Juventus.

28
The shirt number (which he had worn for Sporting Lisbon) Ronaldo asked for when he signed for Manchester United in 2003. Sir Alex Ferguson refused and told him he would play in the famous number seven.

Above: Portugal's captain won his 100th cap for his country against Northern Ireland in 2012.

37.66
Percentage of the total vote Ronaldo received to win the FIFA Ballon d'Or in 2014.

37
Number of Real Madrid hat-tricks claimed by Ronaldo by the end of 2015–16 – breaking Alfredo di Stefano's long-standing club record.

5
The number of times Ronaldo has won the prestigious Ballon d'Or award, given to the world's best player.

17
Ronaldo's goals total in the 2013–14 Champions League, a single-season record.

51
Goals total for Real in 2015–16, the sixth straight season he has passed 50 in all competitions.

1
According to ESPN in 2019, his ranking in the list of the world's most famous athletes.

TRAINING WITH RONALDO

The star may be blessed with incredible natural talent but he knows that means nothing unless he keeps working hard on the training ground.

Ronaldo was a skinny kid when he arrived at Old Trafford in 2003. The club had just spent $19.7 million (£12.24 million) on the teenager and although Sir Alex Ferguson and his coaching staff knew he had the skills to become a star, there were question marks about whether he was strong enough to cope with tough English soccer.

So Ronaldo hit the gym and over the next few seasons spent hours turning himself into a muscular and powerful player. The results were incredible and prove just how seriously he has always taken his training.

But it was not just building muscles that made Ronaldo such a hit at Manchester United. As well as getting stronger, the youngster would spend his spare time watching video clips of soccer legends like Pelé and Johan Cruyff, studying their tricks and techniques so he could make his own game better.

"I am not a perfectionist but I like to feel that things are done well," he once said. "More important than that, I feel an endless need to learn, to improve, to evolve, not only to please the coach and the fans, but also to feel satisfied with myself. It is my conviction that there are no limits to learning, and that it can never stop, no matter what our age."

The striker took his great attitude with him when he signed for Real Madrid and he is famous for staying behind after training sessions to

Above: Practice makes perfect as Ronaldo works on his headers.

Right: Ronaldo warms up with his teammates ahead of another Real Madrid training session.

40

practice his trademark free-kicks, constantly working on adding more swerve, dip, and power to his shots.

Ronaldo also works very hard in training on his finishing. He will repeat one technique such as a near-post volley or back-post header four times before switching to another way of scoring. It's a way of practicing that he learned at Old Trafford and ensures he's always ready when a goal-scoring chance comes along in a match.

"I am not a perfectionist but I like to feel that things are done well... More important than that, I feel an endless need to learn, to improve, to evolve, not only to please the coach and the fans, but also to feel satisfied with myself. It is my conviction that there are no limits to learning, and that it can never stop, no matter what our age."

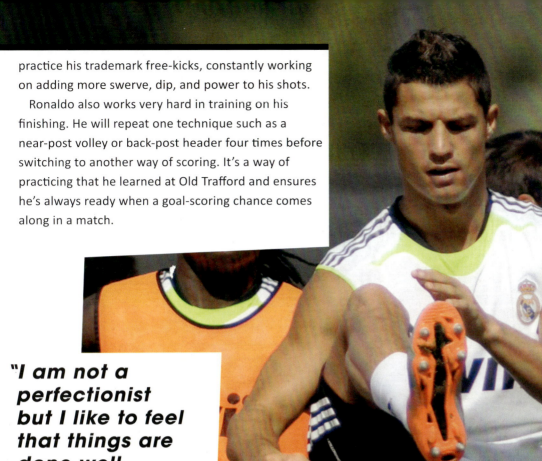

Above: One of the greatest athletes in the game, Ronaldo is always working to get himself in perfect physical condition.

RONALDO'S SUPERSTAR TEAMMATES

Ronaldo was usually surrounded by world-class players during his time at Real Madrid.

GARETH BALE
Signed from Premier League team Tottenham Hotspur for a world record fee in the summer of 2013, the Welsh winger is an amazing natural talent who terrifies defenders with his pace, dribbling ability, and eye for goal. Bale's lethal left foot complemented the right-footed Ronaldo beautifully. The deadly duo were capable of ripping apart even the meanest defenses in La Liga and Europe.

SERGIO RAMOS
The Spanish defender joined the Madrid first team at the start of the 2005–06 season and while Ronaldo scored goals at one end, it is Ramos's job to stop them at the other. Capped more than 100 times by Spain, Ramos can play at both full-back and in central defense and has won three La Liga titles with the club. Fast, strong, and a great reader of the game, he is one of the toughest defenders in world soccer.

LUKA MODRIĆ

If Ronaldo was the man who provides the fireworks at the Bernabéu, it was Modrić who makes the Madrid midfield tick. Signed from Tottenham Hostpur in August 2012, the Croatian maestro initially struggled to find a place in the team under José Mourinho, but flourished under the managerial reign of Carlo Ancelotti. His ability to find the perfect pass for Real's frontmen was evident during Real's march to the Champions League crown in 2014.

TONI KROOS

A World Cup winner in Brazil in 2014, Kroos completed his move to Madrid just four days after Germany had beaten Argentina in the final. A hardworking but creative midfielder at Bayern Munich, he won three league titles and the Champions League before heading to Spain. He missed just eight of 72 La Liga matches in his first two seasons in Madrid and started in the 2016 Champions League final when Real beat Atlético Madrid.

RONALDO AND HIS FANS

One of the most popular players on the planet, Ronaldo is worshipped by millions of supporters all over the world.

If you want an idea just how much Real Madrid supporters love their Portuguese superstar, you only need to watch a video of Ronaldo's official unveiling to the fans in 2009. Eighty thousand people packed into the club's Bernabéu stadium to welcome him to Spain.

Most top European clubs don't even get that many supporters for a match, but Ronaldo was so popular in Madrid that there wasn't a spare seat in the ground when he arrived in Spain – before he had even kicked a ball!

The supporters rushed to buy Real Madrid shirts with Ronaldo's name and number nine on the back (since 2010 he has worn the number seven) and just nine months later the club had sold an unbelievable 1.2 million shirts in Madrid alone. The money made from sales was more than it cost the club to sign the player from Manchester United!

By the end of 2014, Ronaldo shirts were the best-selling replica shirts in the world, beating Barcelona's Lionel Messi into second place.

There are hundreds of unofficial Ronaldo fan clubs around the world and he is one of the most followed people on social media. An astonishing 158 million

Above: The Madrid superstar is a heartthrob as well as a soccer hero.

fans worldwide were following his official Facebook, Instagram and Twitter accounts by 2019.

Ronaldo has repaid his fans many times for their support. In January 2014 he invited a young Real Madrid supporter suffering from cancer to watch a game at the Bernabéu in his own VIP box and in March he agreed to pay $83,000 for another young fan to

Right: Ronaldo's popularity is shown by the millions of replica shirts that have been sold across the globe.

undergo life-saving brain surgery. In February 2016 the Madrid hero celebrated his 31st birthday and to mark his special day he posted a video message to his fans on his Twitter account. "I wanted to thank you for the messages you have sent me," he said. "As you know it's my birthday. Thirty-one years old. So thank you all! We're together. And please keep on supporting me like you do."

Above: Ronaldo makes a Portugal fan's dreams come true by handing him his game shirt after the Euro 2008 match against the Czech Republic.

GREAT PORTUGAL GOALS

The all-time leading scorer for his country, Ronaldo has hit some unbelievable wonder goals while on international duty for his beloved Portugal.

PORTUGAL 7 RUSSIA 1
WORLD CUP QUALIFIER, OCTOBER 13, 2004

There was a stunned silence inside the stadium in Lisbon when Ronaldo scored this wonder goal. He collected the ball just inside enemy territory and, when faced with five Russian defenders, blasted a fierce, dipping drive from outside the area into the top corner.

DENMARK 2 PORTUGAL 1
EURO 2012 QUALIFIER, OCTOBER 11, 2011

His greatest free-kick for his country, this 40-yard effort had everything – power, swerve, and dramatic dip at the end. The ball flew just under the crossbar and into the net.

NETHERLANDS 1 PORTUGAL 2
EURO 2012 GROUP B, JUNE 17, 2012

Ronaldo's two goals fired Portugal into the quarter-finals and his second was a work of art. Collecting a pass from Nani, he dummied a shot that left Dutch defender Gregory van der Wiel on his backside before driving low into the net.

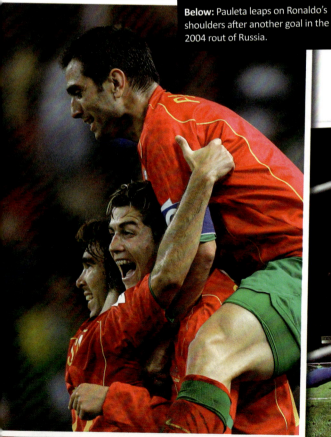

Below: Pauleta leaps on Ronaldo's shoulders after another goal in the 2004 rout of Russia.

Above: Dutch goalkeeper Maarten Stekelenburg is helpless as Ronaldo scores one of his two goals to help Portugal reach the Euro 2012 quarter-finals.

46

SWEDEN 2 **PORTUGAL** 3
WORLD CUP PLAYOFF, NOVEMBER 19, 2013

One of Ronaldo's greatest games for Portugal, his hat-trick booked the team's place in the World Cup Finals. His third goal was a belter as he glided into the Sweden penalty area, expertly took the ball past the goalkeeper, and calmly stroked the ball home.

PORTUGAL 2 WALES 0
EURO 2016 SEMI-FINAL, JULY 6, 2016

The greatest players score when it really matters and Ronaldo did exactly that when he broke the deadlock in the 50th minute of the Euro 2016 semi-final against Wales in Lyon. Full-back Raphaël Guerreiro fired in an accurate, out-swinging cross from the left wing, Ronaldo jumped brilliantly above the Wales defense and powered home a superb header.

Above: The Swedish defense is powerless to stop the striker scoring another wonder goal in the 2014 World Cup qualifying playoff.

Below: Ronaldo's goal against Wales in Euro 2016 was the most important of his record-breaking international career.

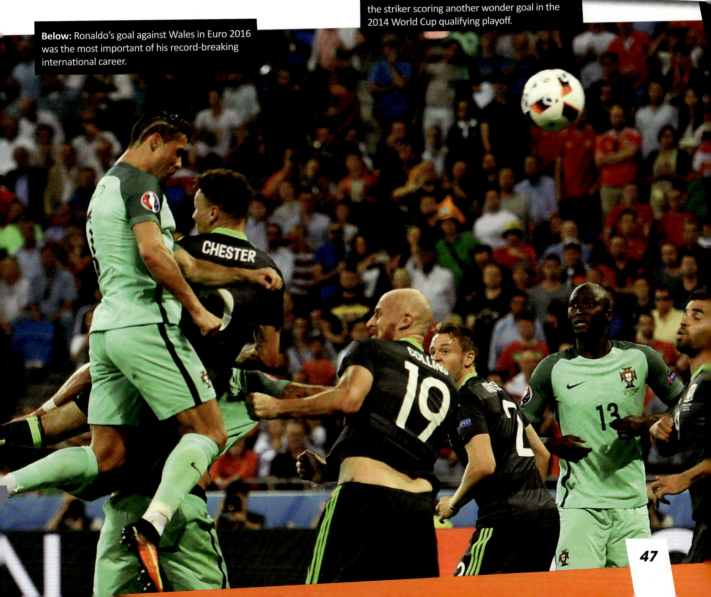

WORLD TRAVELER

Wherever he goes on the planet, Ronaldo is sure to make headlines and is always guaranteed a warm welcome from his fans.

It is a good thing that Ronaldo is not a nervous flyer because the superstar has clocked up thousands of miles in the air since he flew to England to sign for Manchester United back in 2003. There are few countries that he has not yet visited as a soccer player, team captain, charity ambassador, or simply for a vacation.

Modern soccer players travel huge distances to play games and Ronaldo has been as far afield as China with Real Madrid for pre-season tours before returning to Spain for La Liga action.

Real Madrid traditionally set up camp in the USA every summer to get the squad ready for the new season and it was in 2013 that Ronaldo caught up with David Beckham in Los Angeles, a meeting of two of the most famous players in the history of the game.

But it is not just soccer that sees Ronaldo reaching for his passport. The star represents a number of charities and in 2013 he made the journey to Indonesia in his role as an ambassador for the Mangrove Care Forum, an organization that protects the natural environment in the country.

Below: (*from left*) Ronaldo, Iker Casillas, and David Beckham during an airport stopover on Madrid's preseason tour to the United States.

In the same year he also visited a school in Singapore to support the launch of a new scholarship program for talented young athletes.

His soccer and charity work means Ronaldo has a hectic schedule, but there is still time for trips with his children and family. In recent years the striker has jetted off to Miami, Thailand, and St. Tropez to get away from it all.

He certainly deserved a break after inspiring Portugal's incredible victory at Euro 2016 and as soon as the tournament was over Ronaldo headed to a private yacht off Ibiza to relax. But he didn't get an all-over tan because he wore a brace on his left knee to help his recovery from the injury he suffered in the final!

Below: Ronaldo soaks up some rays while on a well-earned vacation.

Above: Ronaldo gets ready to get on another flight with the Portugal national team.

49

EUROPEAN SUPERSTAR

The Champions League is the biggest club competition on the planet and Ronaldo has won it five times in his awesome career.

Cristiano Ronaldo made his Champions League debut for Manchester United against Stuttgart on October 10, 2003, and has gone on to enjoy a remarkable love affair with European soccer's premier club tournament.

His breakthrough season in the competition came in the 2007–08 season. United had lost in the semi-finals the previous year, but with Ronaldo in sensational form they made it all the way to the final to face Chelsea in Moscow, the capital of Russia.

Ronaldo had already scored seven goals on the way to the big match and he was on target again in Russia with an unstoppable first-half header that set up a penalty shootout after extra-time. United held their nerve to be crowned European champions for a third time in the club's history. Ronaldo's haul of eight goals made him the tournament's top scorer.

The striker's next great Champions League season came in 2012–13, when he once again finished as top scorer. Ronaldo fired in an incredible 12 goals, including two in a 3–2 last-16 win over United, as Real Madrid made it to the semi-finals for a second year running.

Ronaldo's form in the 2013–14 tournament was even better. He scored nine goals in the group stages and seven more in the knockout phase as Madrid marched into the final to face city rivals Atlético Madrid.

The final in Lisbon saw Real taken into extra-time by Atlético, but Ronaldo was on target from the penalty spot to seal a famous 4–1 win and secure the second Champions League winner's medal of his amazing career. In total, the striker scored 17 goals in just 11 games – moving to second all-time on the Champions League – as Real ruled Europe for a record 10th time.

Ten titles became a magnificent 11 in 2015–16 as Ronaldo and Real were crowned champions as they again beat Atlético in the final in Rome. The match finished 1–1 and went to a penalty shootout, when it was Ronaldo, naturally, who stepped up to take Real's winning spot-kick.

Real Madrid and Ronaldo made it three in a row by winning the Champions League again in May 2017 and May 2018. Ronaldo extended his record as the top scorer in Champions League history, with 121 goals through the 2017–18 season.

Above: Manchester United's team photo before the 2008 Champions League final against Chelsea.

Above: Ronaldo, who scored in Real's 4–1 win over neighbors Atlético in 2014, shows off the Champions League trophy after becoming one of the few players to be a winner with two clubs.

Below: Ronaldo's penalty in the 2016 final shoot-out ensured he collected his third Champions League winner's medal.

51

RONALDO AND HIS COACHES

The world's greatest soccer player has played for some of the game's finest managers during his record-breaking career.

SIR ALEX FERGUSON

The man who brought him to Manchester United in 2003, Ferguson was a massive influence on Ronaldo's early career. Ferguson was the man who first switched Ronaldo from the wing to striker. Ronaldo then helped the Red Devils win a hat-trick of Premier League titles and the Champions League.

> "I HAVE NOTHING BUT PRAISE FOR THE BOY. HE IS EASILY THE BEST PLAYER IN THE WORLD. HIS CONTRIBUTION AS A GOAL THREAT IS UNBELIEVABLE. HIS STATS ARE INCREDIBLE. STRIKES AT GOAL, ATTEMPTS ON GOAL, RAIDS INTO THE PENALTY BOX, HEADERS. IT IS ALL THERE. ABSOLUTELY ASTOUNDING."
> Sir Alex Ferguson

JOSÉ MOURINHO

The two Portuguese teamed up with spectacular results at Real Madrid between 2010 and 2013 and with the duo together at the Bernabéu, Madrid toppled Barcelona as La Liga champions. Mourinho's famous management skills got the very best out of Ronaldo.

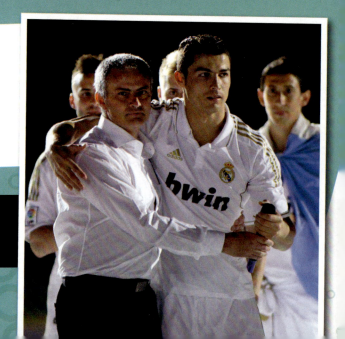

> "IF MESSI IS THE BEST ON THE PLANET, RONALDO IS THE BEST IN THE UNIVERSE."
> José Mourinho

CARLO ANCELOTTI

Another manager at Madrid, the famous Italian has won the league title in Italy, England, and France and Ronaldo grew even more under his leadership. Ancelotti gave the Portuguese star plenty of freedom to attack and Ronaldo responded with some amazing performances for Real.

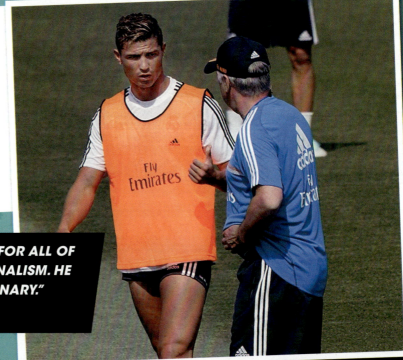

"RONALDO IS A UNIQUE PLAYER FOR ALL OF HIS TALENT AND HIS PROFESSIONALISM. HE IS A PLAYER WHO IS EXTRAORDINARY."
Carlo Ancelotti

ZINEDINE ZIDANE

A Real legend in his own right, the Frenchman became the Bernabéu boss in January 2016 after Rafa Benitez was sacked. Together with his star Portuguese player, he masterminded Real's Champions League triumph. An amazing entertainer in his own playing days, Zidane understands Ronaldo perfectly.

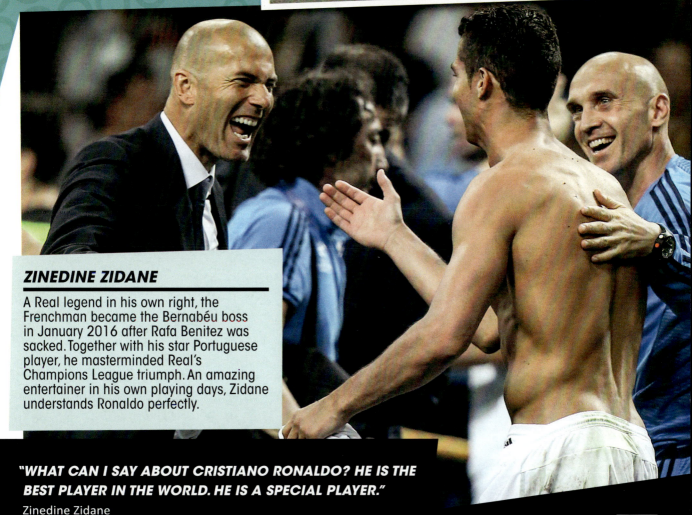

"WHAT CAN I SAY ABOUT CRISTIANO RONALDO? HE IS THE BEST PLAYER IN THE WORLD. HE IS A SPECIAL PLAYER."
Zinedine Zidane

GLOBAL SUPERSTAR

An ambassador for some of the world's biggest brands and the face of Pro Evolution Soccer, Ronaldo even has his own line of clothing and a museum dedicated to him.

Soccer is the most popular sport on the planet and it's no surprise that its greatest player is known all around the world. The striker may be a hero in his native Portugal, but he's just as famous in Peru, the Philippines, and Poland.

"All around the world I have to deal with my fame," Ronaldo said. "I can't go anywhere without being recognized, which can be very hard."

His global reputation has seen the star sign lucrative sponsorship deals with Coca-Cola, men's fashion company Emporio Armani, Motorola, and KFC. He has appeared in a series of TV ads for sportswear giants Nike that have been broadcast all over the world.

In 2006 Ronaldo opened a fashion store called "CR7" (his trademarked initials and shirt number) on the island of Madeira. Two years later he set up a second shop in the Portuguese capital Lisbon.

In December 2013, Ronaldo launched a museum, the Museu CR7, in his hometown of Funchal to celebrate his amazing career. Thousands of fans from all over the world flocked to see the trophies, medals and memorabilia on show, underlining the strength of his global popularity.

The following month he was named the Grand Officer of the Order of Prince Henry by the Portuguese president, an exclusive honor that showed the impact Ronaldo has made in his own country.

The superstar was also honored by the world-famous Madame Tussauds in London when they unveiled a waxwork of him ahead of the 2010 FIFA World Cup. Ronaldo attended the opening ceremony in person with fellow soccer players David Beckham, Pelé, and Steven Gerrard.

In 2014 the famous American magazine *Time* named Ronaldo among the 100 most influential people in the world, while in November 2015, a documentary film about his incredible life and career, called *Ronaldo*, was released in theaters. After Portugal's dramatic win over France in the Euro 2016 final, Madeira Airport in Funchal, his hometown, was renamed Cristiano Ronaldo Airport in honor of his amazing performances in the tournament.

Right: Ronaldo greets the president of Portugal in Lisbon in 2014 when he received his country's equivalent of a knighthood.

Above: Ronaldo's statue at the museum dedicated to him in his native Funchal, Madeira, with the island's capital pictured in the background.

Above: Ronaldo is one of the highest paid athletes signed up by sportswear giant Nike.

RECORD BREAKER

Ronaldo has smashed countless records and reached many marvelous milestones for both club and country during his fabulous career.

Above: Ronaldo celebrates becoming Portugal's all-time leading goal scorer (with 49) after netting a double against Cameroon in March 2014.

Ronaldo has rewritten the record books since he signed for Real Madrid and he is now the fastest player in the club's history to reach the 50, 100, 150, and 200 league goal milestones. He is also the quickest player to reach 200 goals in La Liga history.

The striker jointly holds the record for finding the back of the net in successive Champions League games, scoring in six games in a row for Real Madrid in the competition. His hot streak started with a 4–1 win over Ajax in December 2012 and after finding the back of the net home and away against both Manchester United and Galatasaray (to reach five games in a row), he made it six on the bounce with a goal in the first leg of the semi-final against Borussia Dortmund.

Unstoppable in front of goal for Madrid in 2011–12, he scored a club-record 61 goals in all competitions.

The striker shares the record for the most goals scored in a 38-game Premier League season, hitting the back of the net 31 times in 2007–08. Alan Shearer, for Blackburn in 1995–96, and Luis Suarez, in 2013–14, also scored 31 goals.

The Portuguese set a new record as the first player ever to score in six successive "El Clasico" games between Real Madrid and Barcelona. His amazing run began in the Copa del Rey in January 2012 and carried on until the two teams met in La Liga in October. The remarkable run brought seven goals in six appearances.

Ronaldo is the only man to have won, in a single season, all of: domestic League, Cup, and Super Cup; UEFA Champions League and FIFA Club World Cup; domestic Golden Shoe and Player of the Year; plus Ballon d'Or – World Player of the Year – at two different clubs.

He is only the player to have scored in four European Championship finals (2004, 2008, 2012, and 2016).

In 2015–16 he became the first man ever to grab three Champions League hat-tricks in one season.

Ronaldo has been named in UEFA's Team of the Year 13 times – more than any other player.

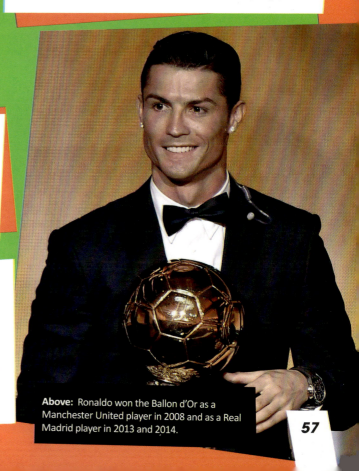

Above: Ronaldo won the Ballon d'Or as a Manchester United player in 2008 and as a Real Madrid player in 2013 and 2014.

WHAT'S NEXT FOR RONALDO?

He has already achieved so much in his years as a professional soccer player, but the ambitious Ronaldo never gets tired of success.

Although he is now in his 30s, Ronaldo is fitter, stronger, and even hungrier for success today than the teenager who first broke into the Sporting Lisbon team back in 2002. Nobody knows how many more records he will break and how many more trophies he will lift before he hangs up his cleats.

After Real Madrid captured their third straight Champions League in May 2018, Ronaldo said, "It has been nice being at Real Madrid." Fans speculated that this meant he was thinking of leaving the club. After the game and in subsequent interviews, he stated that he was excited about Real Madrid's history-making championship and wanted to "enjoy this moment."

But on July 10, Juventus announced that they had signed Ronaldo. The transfer fee was more than $100 million, the highest sum ever paid for a player over 30 years old. The Portuguese star who had already proved himself in the top leagues of England and Spain was headed to Italy to play for the most successful team in Serie A.

Explaining his decision, Ronaldo said he was eager for a new challenge. On one hand, he felt he was not getting as much support from the president of Real Madrid. On the other hand, the leadership at Juventus was thrilled to land one of the best players of all time.

If Ronaldo is lucky with injury, fans can expect to see him continue to dominate his sport for years to come. Playing for Juventus, he will have the opportunity to compete for and win many more league championships and Champions League finals.

Below: The striker is all smiles after winning his 100th cap for Portugal in 2012.

Right: The 2016 Champions League was the eighth trophy of Ronaldo's amazing Real Madrid career.

Above: Ronaldo gives a thumbs-up with Real Madrid president Florentino Pérez.

QUIZ TIME

Here are 20 questions to test just how much you know about Cristiano Ronaldo. All the answers can be found in the preceding pages of this book.

1. On which Portuguese island was Ronaldo born in 1985?
2. What did Ronaldo's mother Maria do for a living?
3. What was the name of the first amateur team he played for as an eight-year-old?
4. How many goals did Ronaldo score on his league debut for Sporting Lisbon?
5. What number shirt did he wear in his one season playing for Sporting Lisbon?
6. How much did Manchester United pay to sign Ronaldo from Sporting Lisbon in 2003?
7. Which player wore the number seven shirt at Old Trafford before Ronaldo joined the club?
8. Against which team did the player make his Champions League debut for United in October 2003?
9. In what year did the forward make his European Championship debut?
10. Against which country did Ronaldo score the winning penalty in the 2006 World Cup quarter-final?

Above: See question 5. Ronaldo made his name for Sporting Lisbon wearing which shirt number?

Above: Ronaldo helps himself to a hat-trick in 2010.

11 How many goals did he score during the 2007–08 Premier League season when Manchester United were crowned champions?
12 Against which team did he score a 40-yard screamer in 2009 to win the first-ever FIFA Puskas Award for the best goal of the year?
13 Ronaldo holds the record for the most goals scored in a Champions League season. How many did he score in 2013–14?
14 What milestone did Ronaldo reach when he scored against Levante in October 2015?
15 How many times has the Portuguese player finished the season as La Liga's top scorer?
16 Whose old record of 127 caps for Portugal did Ronaldo break in 2016?
17 How many goals did the striker score at Euro 2016 as Portugal were crowned champions?
18 How many times has the star been named in the FIFA FIFPro World XI?
19 Which team lost to Ronaldo and Real Madrid in the 2016 Champions League final?
20 When did Ronaldo transfer to Juventus?

ANSWERS – SEE PAGE 64

GLOSSARY

ambassador A representative.

ambitious Wanting to be successful or achieve a goal.

evolve To change in a way that makes one better.

friendly A game between teams that is not part of the regular season or the league or championship play.

instep The part of the top of the foot that is raised and in the middle.

lucrative Profitable.

maestro A person who is a master or an expert in a field, often in an art.

replica A very close copy of something.

successive When something happens one after another; in a row.

treble When a team wins three trophies in a season.

triumph A great victory; also to achieve such a victory.

FOR FURTHER READING

Books

Jökulsson, Illugi. *Cristiano Ronaldo*. New York, NY: Abbeville Press Publishers, 2015.

Jökulsson, Illugi. *Stars of World Soccer*. New York, NY: Abbeville Press Publishers, 2018.

McCollum, Sean. *Full STEAM Soccer: Science, Technology, Engineering, Arts, and Mathematics of the Game*. North Mankato, MN: Capstone Press, 2019.

Porterfield, Jason. *Cristiano Ronaldo: Soccer Champion*. New York, NY: Britannica Educational Publishing, 2019.

Websites

FIFA
www.fifa.com
Find all the most up-to-date news about soccer around the world on FIFA's website.

Juventus
www.juventus.com/en/teams/first-team/forwards/ cristiano-ronaldo/index.php
Keep up with Ronaldo's stats on the Juventus website.

Sports Illustrated Kids
www.sikids.com/soccer
Keep up with the latest happenings in soccer on the Sports Illustrated Kids website.

INDEX

A
Almunia, Manuel, 21
Andorinha, 8, 10
Andorra, 36
Arsenal, 21
Aston Villa, 20
Athletic Bilbao, 24
Atlético Madrid, 24, 25, 43, 50
Aveiro, José Dinis (father), 8, 26
Aveiro, Maria Dolores dos Santos (mother), 8, 10, 26

B
Bale, Gareth, 31, 42
Ballon d'Or, 6, 23, 39, 57
Barcelona, 24, 31, 34, 44, 52
Beckham, David, 14, 48, 54
Boloni, Laszlo, 12
Bolton Wanderers, 22, 28
Borussia Dortmund, 31, 57

C
Champions League, 6, 20, 21, 22, 23, 24, 25, 31, 39, 43, 50, 52, 53, 57, 58
Chelsea, 20, 34, 50
Copa del Rey Final, 24

D
da Silva Ferreira, Eusébio, 16, 17
Debrecen, 22

E
endorsements, 54

European Golden Shoe, 23, 57
European Under-17 Championship, 10

F
Ferguson, Alex, 14
FIFA FIFPro World XI, 39
FIFA Puskás Award, 23
FIFA World Cup, 6, 18, 22, 36, 43, 46, 47, 54, 57
FIFA World Player of the Year, 23, 57
Figo, Luís, 16, 17, 28
"Flip Flap," 32
Football Writers' Association Footballer of the Year, 22
Fulham, 34
Funchal, Madeira, 6, 8, 10, 54

G
Greaves, Jimmy, 25

H
heart condition, 6

J
Juventus, 6, 34, 39, 58

K
Kroos, Toni, 43

M
Malaga, 24
Manchester United, 14, 20, 21, 22, 23, 28, 34, 39, 40, 44, 48, 50, 52, 57
Messi, Lionel, 23, 25, 44

Millwall, 22
Modrić, Luka, 43
Moreirense, 12
Museu CR7, 54

N
Nacional, 10

P
PFA Fans' Player of the Year, 22
PFA Players' Player of the Year, 22
PFA Young Player of the Year, 22
Piqué, Gerard, 31
Porto, 21, 23
Portsmouth, 29
Portugal national team, milestones in Ronaldo's career with, 36, 38, 46–47, 49
Primeira Liga, 12, 13
Puskás, Ferenc, 18

R
Ramos, Sergio, 42
Rayo Vallecano, 30
Reagan, Ronald, 8
Real Madrid, 6, 24, 26, 30, 31, 34, 38, 39, 40, 42, 43, 44, 48, 50, 52, 53, 57, 58
Real Mallorca, 24
Ronaldo, Alana (daughter), 26
Ronaldo, Cristiano, Jr. (son), 26
Ronaldo, Eva (daughter), 26

Ronaldo, Mateo (son), 26

S
Schalke, 25
Spanish Super Cup, 31, 57
Sporting Lisbon, 10, 12, 13, 14, 15, 16, 58

T
training methods, 40–41

U
UEFA Best Player, 25
UEFA Champions League, 6, 20, 22, 23, 24, 25, 28, 29, 57
UEFA European Championships
Euro 2004, 16, 28, 57
Euro 2008, 17, 57
Euro 2016, 6, 17, 29, 47, 49, 57

V
Valdés, Víctor, 31
Villareal, 30

W
Wolfsburg, 25

Z
Zidane, Zinedine, 18, 28, 53

CREDITS

The publishers would like to thank the following sources for their kind permission to reproduce the pictures in this book. The page numbers for each of the photographs are listed below, giving the page on which they appear in the book and any location indicator (T-top, B-bottom, C-center, L-left, R-right).

Cover photo: Marco Iacobucci EPP/Shutterstock. Cover design element: pingebat/Shutterstock.
Getty Images: 49R; /Gonzalo Arroyo Moreno: 53T; /Shaun Botterill: 50, 51BR; /Martin Bureau/AFP: 2; /Victor Carretero: 30L; /City Files/WireImage: 26; /Fabrice Coffrini/AFP: 27R, 57; /Nuno Correia/Allsport: 10R; /Antonio Cotrim/AFP: 13; /Gregorio Cunha/AFP: 8TR, 27BL; /Helios de la Rubia: 24; /Gregg DeGuire/FilmMagic: 41, 48; / Adrian Dennis/AFP: 22L; /Denis Doyle: 9, 25, 30BR, 35, 42BR; /Paul Ellis/AFP: 47B; /Don Emmert/AFP: 55R; /Franck Fife/ AFP: 6L, 22-23, 28BL, 63; /Charley Gallay/FilmMagic: 49BL; /Laurence Griffiths: 15, 51T; /Valery Hache/AFP: 4-5; /Matthias Hangst: 58BR; /Mike Hewitt; /Karim Jaafar/AFP: 19; /Liu Jin/AFP: 44R; /Jasper Juinen: 33R, 40R, 44BR, 61; /Talar Kalajian/AFP: 40BR; /Andre Kosters/AFP: 14L, 54; /Jean-Pierre Ksiazek/AFP: 17; /Christopher Lee: 55L; /Bryn Lennon: 28R; /Francisco Leong/AFP: 29, 52TL; /Jochen Luebke/AFP: 18BL; /Pierre-Philippe Marcou/AFP: 6R, 59; /Angel Martinez: 3; /Jamie McDonald: 21, 46L; /Jonathan Nackstrand/AFP: 47T; /Thomas Niedermueller: 45; /Pedro Nunes/AFP: 56; /John Peters: 14R; /Dani Pozo/AFP: 32; /Cristina Quicler/AFP: 38; /David Ramos: 31B; / Jaime Reina/AFP: 42L, 52BR; /Miguel Riopa/AFP: 20, 39, 58R; /Clive Rose: 33TL; /Martin Rose: 36; /STR/AFP: 16L; / Evaristo Sa/AFP: 18TR; /Antonio Simoes/AFP: 16R, 60; /TF-Images: 31R; /Bob Thomas/Popperfoto: 37; /VI Images: 8BL, 10L, 11, 12, 43R, 53B; /Visionhaus/Corbis: 7, 43BL; /Ian Walton: 46R.

Every effort has been made to acknowledge correctly and contact the source and/or copyright holder of each picture and we apologize for any unintentional errors or omissions that will be corrected in future editions of this book.

ANSWERS

QUIZ TIME

1 Madeira. 2 Cook. 3 Andorinha. 4 Two. 5 28. 6 $19.7 million. 7 David Beckham. 8 Stuttgart. 9 2004. 10 England. 11 31. 12 Porto. 13 17. 14 He became Real's all-time top scorer with 324 goals. 15 Three. 16 Luís Figo. 17 Three. 18 Nine. 19 Atlético Madrid. 20 July 10, 2018.